the Beginning of You

Amy Rebeca Botts

Illustrated by Daniela Cox

Archway Publishing books may be ordered through booksellers or by contacting:

Archway Publishing
1663 Liberty Drive
Bloomington, IN 47403
www.archwaypublishing.com
844-669-3957

ISBN: 978-1-6657-4357-0 (sc)
ISBN: 978-1-6657-4358-7 (hc)
ISBN: 978-1-6657-4359-4 (e)

Library of Congress Control Number: 2023908189

Print information available on the last page.

Archway Publishing rev. date: 05/25/2023

This book is dedicated to everyone who had a beginning.

When you started out,
you were as small as a dot.
you did not seem like much,
but soon you'd be a whole lot!

You started as one. . .

then those

split into two. . .

those two became
four. . .

and four
became more!

And then even more
and more
and more parts

and then all the
mores became
your arms
and legs
and your
heart.

Such wonderful
things happening
so your parts
could form.

Your mommy home was so comfy, and cozy and warm.

After five or so weeks
your heart started
to beat.

The flittery, fluttery
thump-thump was
so sweet!

Soon you'd grow teeny tiny fingers and toes.

and tiny
little nostrils. . .

for your tiny little nose.

Your hands were so little, and your feet were so small and even smaller were your fingernails and eye lashes...

those were the
smallest of all!

Inside your cozy, warm home with your mommy, you could hear laughing and music in her tummy!

You spent your days snoozin' and at night you were movin'. The sound of her heartbeart got you to groovin'

You grew so much,
it was getting harder
to move about.

If you got much
bigger, you'd have
to move out!

Then the
day came...

when it
was time to
come home

To the arms
and the voice
and to the love
that you have
only ever known.

The. . .

Beginning.

Printed in the United States
by Baker & Taylor Publisher Services